Chr. Charles Schieferdeᴄ

Horrors of Vaccination

Chr. Charles Schieferdecker

Horrors of Vaccination

ISBN/EAN: 9783743325401

Manufactured in Europe, USA, Canada, Australia, Japa

Cover: Foto ©ninafisch / pixelio.de

Manufactured and distributed by brebook publishing software
(www.brebook.com)

Chr. Charles Schieferdecker

Horrors of Vaccination

HORRORS

OF

VACCINATION.

BY

Dr. SCHIEFERDECKER.

Quod odi, hoc facio.

NEW YORK:

AMERICAN NEWS COMPANY,

AGENTS FOR THE PUBLISHER,

Nos. 117, 119 & 121 NASSAU STREET.

,1870.

HORRORS OF VACCINATION.

During the late rebellion in the United States, a conspiracy was suspected to introduce infected clothing into the Northern cities and garrisons, for the purpose of accomplishing by disease what the Southerners were unable to accomplish by their arms. When this conspiracy was said to be discovered, it produced a shock not limited to any race or country. It was felt that none but demons could carry on war upon such principles, and that there was no imaginable punishment too severe for it. While we are unable to place any limits to our indignation at such a hideous crime, though perpetrated in the hallowed name of patriotism, we are not only countenancing, but, in some instances, by law compelling the great mass of our population to submit to be poisoned, their blood corrupted, and the foundations laid for the most devastating diseases with which the human family has been scourged.

This systematic poisoning of our race is done in

the name of science; and the vast army of physicians, who ought to protect the public health, are the agents authorized to spread a malignant virus through the world. Not content with infecting the blood of the adult and the aged, they take the helpless infant from its mother's breast, and, with the lancet, transplant a virus, concentrated by disease, into its pure blood, and thus compel it to contend for the rest of its life with diseases which it otherwise would probably never have known.

This method of wholesale devastation, which sends thousands annually to premature graves, which shocks no one, which the law encourages instead of punishing, is called "Vaccination."

It is now about a century and a half since Lady Mary Wortley Montague introduced from the East the system of inoculating with the virus of small-pox as a preventive of that disease. A natural instinct resisted this insane effort to cast out devils by Beelzebub, the prince of devils, but it gained a sufficient footing to demonstrate that it was propagating frightfully the disease it was designed to check. In 1746 a small-pox hospital for inoculating the poor was established in London, and in 1752 the deaths from small-pox were more numerous than ever before.*

Inoculation was prohibited by royal authority in Paris in 1763, in consequence of an investigation which proved that the infection was multiplied and diffused by that process. Moore, in his History of Small-pox, says: "It is asserted in Spaiu, where the practice was scarcely ever admitted, that small-pox has caused less mortality, in proportion to the population, than in any other country in Europe."

In 1768, the Empress Catharine, of Russia, under the advice of Baron Dinsdale, submitted herself and her son Paul to his treatment by inoculation. This high example spread the practice through Russia, and diffused the natural small-pox and all its attendant evils so rapidly that the Imperial Physician makes a calculation by which it appears that in less than twenty-five years every seventh child born in Russia died annually of small-pox.†

Just as common sense was beginning to get the better of this frightful delusion, and about eighty years since, Dr. Jenner introduced, as its substitute, the

---

* Baron's Life of Jenner, p. 233.

† Moore's History of Small-pox, p. 286.

practice of inoculating with virus taken from cows infected with-pox, instead of that taken from small-pox patients. He pretended that the virus from cows developed a more mitigated form of disease than inoculation, and was equally efficient as a prophylactic. This more dangerous, because less readily detected, delusion, though very justly denounced by his contemporaries as an attempt to beastialize the human race, and diabolical in its tendencies, has grown in favor with the world, until now vaccination in many countries is enforced by law ; and all the foul diseases, of which it is the vehicle, are diffused among men, not only with the sanction, but at the expense of many of their governments.

In 1845, while I was the Medical Director of a water-cure establishment in Philadelphia, I was cognizant of the case of a lady in that city, of feeble health, who had been repeatedly vaccinated, being restored to perfect health by a violent attack of confluent small-pox. I myself, though I had been vaccinated several times, also took the disease, which attacked every patient in my establishment who had been vaccinated. Only one, a Mr. J. Kay, who had never been vaccinated, escaped.

These most unexpected results led me to investigate the theory upon which inoculation and vaccination, as prophylactics, have been commended to the world. My investigations have brought me to the following conclusions:

1. That it is not true that vaccination is a preventive of small-pox. '

2. That cow-pox virus is as decided a poison as that taken from the small-pox patient.

3. That vaccination propagates a variety of other diseases, many of which are more fatal than small-pox, such as scarlet-fever, croup, typhoid-fever, scrofula, consumption, syphilis, cancer, tuberculous formations, diphtheria, etc.

4. That small-pox, as well as other diseases, when they fasten upon people who have been vaccinated, arc more malignant and more difficult to cure than when they attack persons who have never had their blood thus corrupted.

5. That longevity has diminished since the introduction of vaccination.

I.

It is not true that vaccination is a preventive of small-pox.

Independent of my own experience, which has been very far from confirming the pretensions of the disciples of Dr. Jenner, I will cite some of the leading authorities upon this subject. Dr. Pearce, who was for thirty-five years vaccine physician in Edinburgh and London, asks: " How can the historian fall into the error of ascribing the changed mortality from small-pox to vaccination ? In the first thirty years of the last century there died of 1000 small-pox patients, 74; in the last thirty years of the same centutury, after inoculation, there died of 1000, 95." In the Vaccine Report of 1803, it is declared: " It is not at all proved that the vaccine is a benefit for the people, for of about 1000 persons vaccinated, six died and twenty-five suffered from severe illness; while at the same time vaccination spread the contagion and increased the mortality. Of 298 vaccinated, there died in the small-pox hospital in London not less than 31. Consumption increases fearfully." Alexander von Humboldt says, in a letter to Mr. Gibbs, President of the Anti-Vaccine League in London, "that he had clearly perceived the progressive, dangerous influence of vaccine in France, England, and Germany."

During the first years of our century only 15,000, and up to 1808 only about 160,000, individuals were vaccinated in England. If such limited vaccination among a population of nearly twenty millions produced the miraculous effect commonly pretended, why does the disease exist there at all, now that compulsory vaccination is introduced?

In no country is statistical science more advanced than in France, and the Report on the Results of Vaccination of 1865, laid before the Academy in Paris, presents the following facts:

"In ten departments, where, at an average, 28 per cent are vaccinated: cases of small-pox, 1.69 per cent; deaths from small-pox, 9.62 per cent. In ten department, where 100 per cent are vaccinated: cases of small-pox, 10.64 per cent; deaths from small-pox, 9.90 per cent. Or, departments where vaccination is below 50 per cent: cases of small-pox, 2.22 per cent; deaths, 0.17 per cent; and where it is above 50 per

1*

cent, cases of small-pox, 5.69 per cent; deaths, 0.52 per cent."

Marc D'Espine shows, in *Echo Medical*, Juillet, 1859, that of vaccinated people, 65 per cent, and of not vaccinated, only 23 per cent were attacked by the most malignant form of small-pox. Where, from want of physical strength, the pox did not break out, there died of 100 vaccinated, up to 56 per cent; while, according to Perrin, of such not vaccinated, only 8 per cent died at the Hôtel Dieu.

The Report of the Epidemiological Society in London declares, as a proof of the value of vaccination, that before the compulsory vaccination law of 1853, in England, there died of small-pox, during twelve years, 82,825 persons; and after 1853, in the same period, there died only 47,710 persons of the same disease. Let us examine the report:

First. It is thus established, that during twenty-four years, in which vaccination was more or less general, 130,535 persons died of small-pox, and that, therefore, at the average of 7 per cent, which was the average of deaths from this disease prior to the introduction of inoculation, about two millions were attacked by small-pox.

Second. The same report shows, that whenever the small-pox decreased, other skin-diseases increased ; so that, notwithstanding the decrease of small-pox after 1853, upward of 100,000 people more died of measles, scarlet fever, whooping cough, and croup, than ever before.

Third. It also proves that nearly 230,000 more people died of consumption than before.

Fourth. Of the small-pox patients, about 84 per cent were vaccinated, and 16 per cent were not vaccinated.

Fifth. It is a fact that in London there had not been a real small-pox epidemic from 1796 to 1825 ; but since the general introduction of vaccination, not one year has been entirely exempt from the disease ; and during the years from 1863 to 1865, there died in London alone, of small-pox, more than 20,000 persons.

It is also known that, during the years from 1863 to 1865, small-pox prevailed to an enormous extent, not only in England, but also in Germany, Hungary, France, and Sweden, notwithstanding the general compulsory vaccination. In Upper-Bavaria, where the compulsory law is strictly executed, there were, at the time 1346, attacked by malignant small-pox, 1256 vaccinated, and 90 not vaccinated; so that vaccination has not even made the disease milder.

We know further, that the average of deaths from small-pox was in former times about 7 per cent; whereas Dr. Bayard, an eminent French physician, shows that now generally 15 to 20 per cent die.

Dr. Engel, the head of the Bureau of Statistics in Berlin, proves, from a careful calculation, extending over forty-three years, "that death by small-pox, on the whole, occurs now as frequently as formerly."

Dr. Collins, twenty years vaccine physician in London and Edinburgh, writes: "There really exists no change in the virulent character of the small-pox, notwithstanding the vaccination-laws; and of those attacked by the disease, at least two-thirds were satisfactorily vaccinated." He adds: "If I had the desire to describe one-third of the victims ruined by vaccination, the blood would stand still in your veins. . . . . . We have to discern between two classes received in our institute: 1st, People who live in well ventilated houses, who are well dressed and fed and cared for; these are the vaccinated ones. And 2nd, People who live in the very opposite conditions, who stand lower in a physical and mental point of view, and have consequently less life-power; these are the not-vaccinated. I have not the least confidence in vaccination; it nauseates me, for it transfers often filthy and dangerous diseases from one to another, without offering any protection whatever."

Statistical tables further show that, from 1675 to 1761, the yearly average deaths by small-pox were, in London, 7 per cent; in Edinburgh, 7.6 per cent; in Paris, 7.2 per cent; in Berlin, 8.1 per cent. The small-pox killed before inoculation from 7 to 8 per cent; of those attacked by it under inoculation, the mortality increased to from 7 to 10 per cent, and vaccination has elevated this rate to from 11 to 15 per cent. The disease reached its acme in 1779 and 1784, and then for fifteen years grew slowly milder, and in 1809 it nearly disappeared; but in its stead, a typhoid (variola intestinalis) developed itself, which yearly snatched away many thousands more than any epidemic of small-pox. Besides this, some of the greatest lights of the faculty have observed and declare, " that people who are not vaccinated, far more readily recover from any acute disease than those who are vaccinated."

II.

While it is established upon perfectly competent authority that vaccination is not a reliable prophylactic, I propose now to show upon equally good authority,

1st, *That the cow-pox virus is as decided a poison as that taken from a small-pox patient; and,*

2nd, *That its introduction into the human system propagates a variety of other diseases, many of which are more fatal than small-pox, such as scarlet fever, croup, typhoid fever, scrofula, consumption, syphilis, cancer, tuberculous formations, diphtheria, etc.*

I.—Cow-pox is Poisonous.

The highest legal authorities define poison to be not only corrosive and caustic matters in general, which in certain known quantities endanger the health and life of an individual, but all matters which, when introduced into the body, secretly effect its destruction. The cow-pox therefore is a poison, (1,) Because it is the product of infectious matter of a corrosive character, for it produces on the sexual organs of the cow inflammation and suppuration;

(2,) Because in certain quantities it endangers the health and life of children; (3,) Because, like syphilitic poison, it causes inflammation and ulcers. It was for these reasons precisely that inoculation was forbidden in many parts of Europe, and is now discountenanced by the medical profession everywhere. Why is not vaccination also? It is now ascertained that the cow-pox does not originate with the cow, but is probably communicated to it by the infected hand of the milker, for there is no case on record, that I am aware of, of a bull or ox having the pox.*

Dr. Stamm, most careful observer, and author of a Treatise on Animal Virus, declares that he never succeeded in finding a single cow in which the pox had originated. Vaccine, therefore, is simply human small-pox strained through the system of the cow or some other animal, and is as much an animal virus as syphilis, malanders, scarlet-fever, cholera, or hydrophobia, etc. Then, why not inoculate for them? There have been physicians, among whom are Doctors Turenne, Froriep, and Tardieu, who recommend

---

* The scarcity of cow-pox has frequently led to the use of virus taken from the diseased feet of horses (malanders), also from sheep. It is all called "genuine vaccine."

inoculation for these diseases also; but the medical
faculty generally, who are so persistent in poisoning
to prevent small-pox, have hitherto shrunk from the
logical consequences of their theory when it is proposed to apply it to other and kindred maladies.
This, in itself, is the best possible evidence that they
know not what they do; that they are working in
the dark; that they have created in the popular mind
expectations which they dare not admit their inabil-
ity to satisfy.

II.—Vaccination propagates a large Variety of
    other Diseases more dangerous than Small-
    pox.

I will first cite the authority of a prominent champion of vaccination, Dr. Hoffert, of Dantzic. In a
" Review of the Principal Objections to Vaccination," he regrets that small-pox frequently attacks
vaccinated persons, (p. 24;) but parries the effect of
this admission by suggesting that small-pox itself oc-
casionally occurs a second time in the same person,
(p. 26;) that the increase of the small-pox is the consequence of unskillful vaccination, the use of bad
lymph, (p. 31,) a too small number of incisions;

(p. 36,) "but here exists a great diversity of opinion."
He acknowledges that *impetigo* has been transferred
by vaccination, (p. 42 ;) that scrofula may be developed, (p. 44 ;) that syphilis has been thus transplanted, (p. 45 ;) "that the greatest care will not prevent
the possibility of such poisoning by vaccination," (p.
51 ;) and, finally, "now that small-pox has ceased
among children, many who would have died of small-
pox, die of measles, scarlet-fever, and similar diseases,
which have become more malignant," (p. 53.)

An attempt was made in 1853 to pass a law in the
British Parliament making vaccination compulsory,
with partial success. In 1855, Dr. Simon, who had
voted against the law, was commissioned to get the
opinion of the highest medical authorities in and out
of England on the question and report thereon to
Parliament. He addressed 539 physicians, *all sup-
posed by him to approve of vaccination.* Of the 539
answers received, 235 were simply "Yes," or "No,"
72 permit vaccination with the genuine Jenner blis-
ter only, 16 give vaccination their unconditional ap-
proval, 216 offer the following objections to vaccination :

1. It directly endangers life.

2. It nurses and developes latent diseases.

3. Children frequently do not thrive so well after as before vaccination, especially during teething, change of teeth, and puberty.

4. It introduces new diseases into the system of the vaccinated patient.

In spite of this formidable array of authority against vaccination, the English Parliament renewed the law for compulsory vaccination in 1858, by a vote of 101 to 95.

A system of protection, which recommends itself so imperfectly to the judgment of professional observers, after an experience of seventy years, is certainly not worthy of legislative sanction; still less of being imposed upon that half of the community who regard it justly as no better than legalized poisoning.

Dr. Mitchell introduced into Parliament, in the vain effort to arrest the progress of this mad legislation, a protest numerously signed, couched in the following terms:

"We protest against the transplantation of an animal virus, taken from a diseased brute, into the blood of our children; the operation is nauseating, barbarous, and unnatural. It is our opinion, that the purity of the blood is the supreme basis of our well-being; but it is made impure, and becomes the source of diseases, when it is mixed with this beastly poison.

" It is asserted, that the animal virus, when mixed with the pox-poison in the blood, destroys the latter, or that both destroy themselves mutually. We cannot believe this assertion, because it is not only irrational, but because it contradicts all our knowledge of the influence of matter upon matter, when it pretends that, in consequence of the mixture of two corrupt animal substances, the newly gained product becomes pure and innocuous.

" Even if we assume that this new product did possess neither the characteristics of cow-pox nor those of small-pox, it, being another kind of corrupt matter, must necessarily have a corrupting and diseasing influence."

Dr. Hebra, professor of Therapeutics at Vienna, and author of a " Manual on Skin Diseases," enumerates some twelve life endangering, anomalous diseases liable to occur to a person under vaccination. He also, though a champion of vaccination, admits that the small-pox is liable to recur, and that the second attack is very much more dangerous than the first. Notwithstanding he recommends that small-pox be taken by vaccination, he acknowledges that it will often not prevent a recurrence of the disease, and if it does recur, that it is more difficult to treat it than at the first attack.

Professor Bock, in Leipzig, in answer to the question : "Is vaccination advantageous or otherwise?" replied : "I have, in a forty years practice, seen far more evil than good from vaccination, and therefore vaccinated my own children only in their third and fourth year, when they were hearty and strong. But I would never have vaccinated them, but for an indirect compulsory vaccination. It cannot be doubted that a kind of *pyæmia* (poisoning of the blood) is caused by vaccination in the infantile organism, even if the vaccine lymph be taken from perfectly healthy children, or from cows, and it is proved that such a blood poisoning certainly also may have very bad consequences. I would, therefore, never vaccinate a nursing baby in the first months of its life, and far less at the time of its weaning or teething."

Dr. Stowell, for twenty years vaccine physician in

England, says : " The nearly general declaration of
my patients, enables me to proclaim that vaccination
is not only an illusion, but a curse to humanity.
More than ridiculous, it is irrational to say, that
any corrupt matter taken from boils and blisters of
an organic creature could affect the human body,
otherwise than to injure it. First it was asserted
that vaccination protected for life. When this proved
a failure, revaccination in every seventh year was
proposed ; but this also failed. Then there was a
want of sufficient cow-pox. Well, cows were inoculated with human pox, and the suppurated matter
produced by this operation was called pox-lymph,
fresh from the cow. This bastard poison is now
transferred into human bodies, no matter what man
or brute may have been afflicted with ; but it is
called now-a-days " genuine vaccine." This " pure "
lymph is carried from child to child, and spreads a
diseased condition, so that hospitals and drug-shops
have increased eighty per cent, and continue to do
so from day to day. What are 450 physicians of
the Blue-Book, while there are in London alone
3000 physicians ? I, myself, know more than a hundred physicians who think like me."

Dr. Skelton says: "I have belonged many years to the great army of vaccinators, but cannot take any longer upon myself the responsibility connected with the operation, because vaccine does not only not protect, but it also produces other diseases."

Dr. Epps, twenty-five years director of the Jenner Institute, had vaccinated about 120,000 persons, but finally declared: "The vaccine-virus is a poison. As such, it penetrates all organic systems, and infects them in such a way as to act repressively on the pox. It is neither antidote nor corrigent, nor does it neutralise the small-pox, but only paralyzes the expansive power of a good constitution, so that the disease falls back upon the mucous membranes. Nobody has the right to transplant such a mischievous poison compulsorily into the life of a child."

In England there were in 1841, 58,000 cases of small-pox, and 301,788 of scarlet, measles, cholera, whooping cough; and in 1851, only 38,275 cases of small-pox, but 503,467 of scarlet, measles, &c.; so that, while small-pox had decreased about 20,000, the other acute diseases had increased about 200,000.

III.

Dr. Vilette de Terzé proves, in his *La Vaccine, ses consequenses funestes*, (Paris 1857), that "Typhus, scrofula and tubercles are transformed internal small-pox."

Dr. Pearce said, in a meeting at Northampton on the 22d of May, 1860 : "I have, in all regions where vaccination is compulsory, observed an increase of mortality. The general report proves, that whenever smallpox was increasing, other diseases decreased, and whenever the smallpox decreased, other, mostly more fatal diseases increased."

Dr. Perrin, a prominent French physician, says that the influence of vaccination on mortality was proved in 1854, in France. He mentions 114 cases of typhus ; of these 76 were vaccinated, and of them 35 died ; of the other 38, not vaccinated, only three died. Baron Michel shows in his statistical report of the 25,000 soldiers in Paris (from the hospital Gros Caillou), that the mortality is doubled since vaccination, and that fevers have increased six fold.

Dr. Bayard, in a report to Parliament, calls vaccin

ation "a crime against nature. The spreading of
the virus coincides with the predisposition of the
human family to boils, putridity, or brute disease.
Vaccination only retards the small-pox, but does not
extinguish it, and has, at least, doubled the mortality
among young people."

Dr. Schlegel, Professor at Altenburg, in Saxony,
finds that the number of unfortunates who suffer
from affections of the eyes, ears, speech and mind,
are infinitely greater now than before vaccination.

Dr. Plagge, in *Sources of Insanity*, observes that
the causes of increasing suicide and of insanity are
not so much to be searched in social conditions, but
in the terrible progress of the corruption of the human fluids.

France had, in the year 1851, 40,970 insane, and
70,066 mentally imbecile individuals. If prominent
authors on insanity, such as Kelp, Eulenburg, Erlen-
mayer, Otto, Berklau, tabulate seventy-one cases of
insanity as a direct consequence of vaccination, why
should we not have the right to assume that this operation is the most prolific cause of the fearful increase of madness, particularly as the fact cannot
otherwise be satisfactorily explained?

One horrible result of vaccination is now established beyond doubt, viz: the transplantation and spreading of syphilis, cancer, scrofula, tubercular disease, &c. Dr. Ricord declared in 1862 : " If there should be the fact indisputably established that by vaccination even only in one case syphilis is transferred, vaccination must cease." On the 10th of May, 1863, he exclaimed before the Academy at Paris : " First I rejected the idea that syphilis could be transplanted by vaccination. But facts accumulated more and more, and now I must concede the possibility of the transfer of syphilis by means of vaccine. I do this reluctantly. But I do not hesitate any longer to acknowledge and proclaim the reality of the fact." Prof. Depaul, Director of Vaccine in Paris, reported to the Academy 450 cases of vaccine-syphilis. The before mentioned and latest vaccine-champion, Dr. Hoffert, concedes, " that the vaccinator, with all caution, will not always be able to prevent the syphilitic poisoning," and adds: " I have no doubt that syphilis has been transplanted by vaccination, as long as vaccination is the property of the people."

Dr. Heim, the most prominent vaccinator of Wur-

2

temberg, coolly declares, "that the most expert di-
agnostician will not always be able to discover dys-
cracies in vaccine children, and that he himself has
transplanted syphilis from a child which seemed to
him perfectly healthy." Forty-eight physicians tes-
tify in the Blue Book to the same effect.

The vaccinator Borham acknowledges in a letter
to Lord Lyttleton, "that the lymph taken from an
unhealthy person was a dangerous poison, the effect
of which showed itself soon in loathsome eruptions,
and laid the foundation of scrofulous and tubercular
diseases."

Dr. Copland, in his Dictionary, says, "that it is
certain that scrofulous and tubercular diseases have
increased since the introduction of cow-pox, and
that the vaccine favors particularly the prevalence
of various forms of scrofula." Niemeyer, a champion of vaccination, acknowledges, "that cow-pox
leaves scrofulous affections behind." Similar testimony is given by Giraudeau de St. Gervais, Hufe-
land, Hertwig, Most, Grisolle, Canstatt, Bednar, and
others, *who count up some thirty more or less dangerous diseases, as direct consequences of vaccination.*

Prof. Hamernick, of Prague, before the Bohemian

Legislature, called "vaccination a disgrace for the medical practice."

Prof. Ennemoser writes about vaccination : "A more infernal mystification the world has never experienced since its existence ; the belief in witches can only be compared with it. It is certainly not to be comprehended how a poison in the organism can be extinguished by a similar poison." Prof. Kranichfeld, of Berlin, exclaims : "I, too, have vaccinated my fourteen children at a time when I did not know how injurious it was ; to-day I would resist the authorities and the police-law." Prof. Hochstetter, of Esling, declares : "The very Blue Book, which is quoted as a testimony in favor of vaccination, has created in me the gravest doubts. The Blue Book is for every one who reads it carefully the strongest proof against vaccoination."

Dr. Verde de Lisle, an eminent French physician, says : "How is it that in an enlightened century the Academy of Medicine, which is the centre and stimulus of this great question, tries to support a pitiable prejudice, not by solid and uncontrovertible reasons, but pomposity, prizes, medals and admonitions ? It is high time for the interest of sci-

ence and humanity to stop and show how this mad,
beastly corruption of the blood has injured our race.
It is high time for the Academy to take up this
question among its labors, if it would not burden
itself with a heavy responsibility for all the misery
with which vaccine has already afflicted from three
to four generations. It is time to examine whether
Jenner and his consorts, in order to have their so-
called protective remedy against small-pox adopted,
had the dishonest view to deceive the government
and public about the real nature of their specific.
In case of affirmative answer we will ask the Academy :

"1. Whether, by the transplantation of a skin-disease from an animal to the human being, other affections besides the skin-disease are not transferred?

"2. Whether, in consequence of the transfer of
such a skin-disease, the absorbing and resorbing abil-
ity of the skin-vessels are not partly destroyed?

"3. Whether, in consequence of this effect, the
loathsome eruptive matters, destined by nature to be
thrown out of our economy, do not find an insur-
mountable barrier in the skin, and are therefore com-
pelled to show themselves in the interior in various

forms, and whether these obvaccinal disorganizations arc not infinitely more serious, and a hundred times more fatal than the natural smallpox, which the vaccine poisoning is to avoid?

" 4. Whether the number of these diseases, which have so luxuriantly grown since the introduction of vaccine, are not the effects of vaccination ?"

Dr. Mitchell said, in a speech in the lower House of Parliament, " that vaccine has made murder legal. Vaccination did not protect against small-pox, but was followed by blindness and scrofula. Jennerism is the most colossal humbug which the human race has been burdened with by fraud and deceit."

It has been shown by Professor Langenbeck, Lebert and Follin, that not only syphilis, but also cancer can be transplanted ; and by Villemin, Cornil, Simon and others, that the same can be done with tubercles.

IV.

When small-pox, as well as other diseases, fasten upon vaccinated patients, they are more malignant and more difficult to treat than when they attack those whose blood has never been thus corrupted.

I have already cited numerous authorities covering this point; I will cite some others.

Dr. C. T. Pearce writes, on the 10th of August, 1867, to Dr. Stowell, and through him to Lord Lyttelton: "Since 1860 I observe, more and more, that the prospects of recovery of fever-patients are far greater with the not vaccinated than with the vaccinated. I have made a terrible experience. The small-pox broke out in the Metropolitan Hospital. Four nurses, three of whom were properly vaccinated, and one not at all, were attacked by the disease. The former three suffered from the most malignant form, and the latter was only very lightly afflicted. A year later the scarlet-fever broke out, the former three died, and the latter, who was never vaccinated, recovered very easily."

Dr. Gregory, for fifty years Director of the Small-pox House in London, published, before his death, in the *Medical Times* of January 27th, 1852, his opinion that the "idea of extinguishing the small-pox by vaccination is as absurd as chimerical; it is as irrational as presumptuous. I am driven to the conclusion that the susceptibility to pox-miasma grows with years in those who are vaccinated, while the opposite is the case with those not vaccinated, whose susceptibility is greatest in childhood." Gregory refused to have his children vaccinated.

It seems to be the decided conviction of many of the experienced vaccinators, whose opinions I have already cited in this paper, that vaccination fastens the pox-poison on to the mucous membrane. Small-pox eruptions are found in the inner coatings of the body. The intestinal membranes of persons who have died of abdominal typhus are covered with such eruptions, and there exists an intimate connection between this species of typhus and cholera. There is no doubt in my mind that the cholera falsely styled "Asiatic," is one of the consequences of vaccination. There is no reason for calling it Asiatic.

The mere resemblance of certain symptoms of a disease we now have, to a disease which originated thousands of years ago in the valley of the Ganges, from purely local causes, is certainly no reason to assert its importation. Have we not had, for many centuries, the same connection with the East Indies we have now? Why should the year of 1830 be the very precise time when the scourge should have been imported into all civilized and vaccinated countries? The faculty gives frequently very stupid and senseless names; as, for instance, rabies is called Hydrophobia, although the sufferer has really no aversion to water; and to prevent popular prejudices caused by such misnames, Fuchs proposes to call the disease what it is, Dermo-Pneuma-Tetanus. Why not call Asiatic Cholera what it really is, "Intestinal-Pox," caused by vaccination, which, according to above mentioned authorities, acts repressively upon the small-pox, and thus encumbers the inner coating, and predisposes them to the disease?

Dr. Powell, the Health Officer of San Francisco, expressed his astonishment recently at the dreadful ravages and virulent character of the small-pox now a-days. He is dumbfounded at the enormous proportion of deaths to the number of cases, and at the increasing ravages of disease in defiance of the progress of science. Let him follow vaccination in its travels through the blood of the human race, and he will learn the secret of a phenomenon, before which he may well stand appalled.

The fruits of vaccination in England, have recently taken to themselves new terrors. The London Correspondent of the New York *Times* of Dec.

4th, writes : "I fear this letter will seem too full of fault-finding, but there is another subject of very great interest, and which may become so in America as well as in England. We remember something of the ship fever that came to us with the crowds flying from the Irish famine. It was a real famine fever; and such a fever is now increasing in the poorer and more crowded parts of London. It is called the relapsing fever—a form of typhus. It may be carried abroad by emigration, assisted by the government or by parish authorities. The deaths last week, from this and scarlet fever, raised the mortality of the metropolis considerably above the usual rate."

How long will the physicians of London be in discovering that this "famine fever" is another of the blessed results of vaccination?

V.

Longevity has diminished since the introduction of vaccination.

This proposition can scarcely need any farther confirmation than may be found in the facts already cited.

We will quote, however, a few statistics to prove

2*

that everywhere the number of men unfit for mili-
tary service for the last thirty years, has constantly
increased.   Dr. Munaret, a surgeon in the French
army, says, " *Les nombres des impropres au service
militaire va en s'accroisant, j'en accepte les chiffres
et les deplore.*"

Dr. Poche, of the Bureau of Statistics in Austria,
Dr. Wappaeus, Army Surgeon in Prussia, and the
Wurtembergian physicians, complain of the same
facts.   Everywhere the standard measure of the con-
scripts had to be reduced, and is continually reduced.
Dr. Ancelon declares, that the mortality of soldiers
is doubled within the last twenty years.   He adds :
"I have vaccinated for twenty years.   You all have,
I think, vaccinated with enthusiasm.   Why does the
lancet now drop from our hands ?   We blush and
are confounded, because we have not yet, after a
practice of sixty-five years, solved the preliminary
questions : What is vaccine ?   Can it fulfill what it
promised ?   What are its effects ?   We really do not
yet know anything about what Dr. Lalagade calls
'the   divine   element   of   this   precious   preserva-
tive !' "   .

Dr. Engel, Director of Statistical Bureau in Berlin,

states, that the average lifetime has constantly sunk during the last forty years.

Dr. Czoernig, Director of Statistical Bureau in Vienna, declares the same fact, and Dr. Huebner shows that there were in Austria—

1809 to 1828,	to 100 births,	71.9	deaths.
1829 to 1838	" "	86.6	"
1839 to 1843	" "	78.3	"
1850 to 1856	" "	92	"

The "Moniteur," (13th of July, 1862,) proves, that in twenty-nine departments the population is constantly decreasing, which is confirmed by Legoyt, Director of Statistical Bureau in Paris, and by Noirot. Carnot says : "The mortality of people of 20 to 40 years, from 1841 to 1859, increased from 77 to 154."

VI.

It will be apparent to the unprejudiced reader, from the facts I have stated, and the authorities I have cited, that vaccination is not worthy of the confidence which it enjoys from the public, nor the support which it receives from the faculty. The time is not far distant when it will experience the fate which

overtook its parent delusion, inoculation, which was
as much commended in the last century as vaccination in this, but which subsequently, and after a reign
of eighty years, fell under the ban of the law.

Already the power of this new despot is beginning
to shake. Leading physicians, though not daring to
pronounce against vaccination, become daily less and
less disposed to undertake its public defense. Anti-
vaccination Leagues are forming in all parts of Europe ; several European sovereigns have forbidden
re-vaccination in their armies; the English Government has recently directed its minister at the Court
of Wurtemberg to collect all the proofs developed
against vaccination, and to ask Dr. Nittinger, Professor of Pathology at Stuttgart, and the author of a
remarkable work entitled, " Fifty Years of Vaccine
Poisoning," to prepare a memoir upon the subject, to
be laid before the Parliament.

On the 12th of October, 1868, the centennial an-
niversary of the inoculation of the Empress Catharine, the Russian Medical Council offered a prize of
3,000 roubles for the best treatise on the most proper
measures for the prevention of small-pox epidemics,
and diminishing their mortality ; also on the various

methods of vaccination, with a critical examination of their value. Here is their programme:

1. A history of the most important pox-epidemics, and a history of vaccination, with a consideration of the laws of the different governments referring to it, and all the regulations now existing.

2. Present proofs that vaccination is a secure remedy against natural small-pox. Whether it be worth while to consider the assertion made by some physicians, that vaccination favors the spreading of some epidemic diseases.

3. Whether vaccination protects, if at all, for ever, or only for a certain time? What are the conditions of the different degrees of immunity from the pox contagion? With a critical examination of vaccinated persons who were attacked and died of small-pox.

4. What is the normal course of the vaccine pustule, and what the abnormal, with proofs of the existence of a protective infection of the organism? Morphological and other analyses of the vaccine-lymph, which show the infecting matter in it.

5. Can vaccination transplant into the organism other disease germs, and which?

6. A critical examination of all the modes of vaccination before and after Jenner, up to the present
day, (including Equination and Ovination.) It is de-
sirable that the conclusions of the authors be founded
upon their own experimental observation.

7. In what manner can the lymph be best collected
and preserved? What is the duration of its efficacy
and the best manner of sending it to remote regions.
Technics and Hygiene of vaccination.

8. What are the best means of diffusing vaccination ?

9. What evidence is there of the utility of compulsory vaccination and re-vaccination ?

10. Of the erection of vaccine-institutes, as sources
of good lymph and means of spreading vaccination.

It is certainly a remarkable circumstance that so
much money and glory as would reward the successful competitor should not yet have tempted any of
the vast army of vaccinators to come forward and
give to the Russian Medical Council and the world
their reasons for the faith which is in them. If vaccination proves in their practice what Jenner and his
disciples claim it to be, it should be an easy matter
to answer the important question submitted by the

Russian Council, and receive the 3000 roubles as well as the decorations from the Emperor Alexander, which unquestionably await the successful respondent.

Vaccination would long since have gone to the limbo reserved for the innumerable medical quackeries which succeed each other in the world, but for the terrors with which ignorance and an almost insane mode of treating the small-pox had invested that disease. People say that anything which diminishes the risk of taking such a malady is a mercy, and they have been persuaded that vaccination does that at least, never thinking of the more serious diseases which replace it. The small-pox derived the larger part of its horrors in the last century from the frequent bleeding, exhausting heat, and stifling fumigations with which it was treated by the physicians. It is by no means a difficult disease to cure, and I marvel that the medical faculty does not spend more time in searching for a proper hygiene system for the treatment of the small-pox, and less in poisoning the blood of the human family in the absurd attempt to prevent its attacks.

Why is it that such authorities as Currie and Bate-

man, so readily obeyed in other matters, are not also
respected when they enthusiastically praise cold water
as the only safe remedial agent in this class of diseases.
Bateman, in his work entitled "A Practical Synopsis
of Cutaneous Diseases," remarks : " After the extensive evidence, which a period of more than twenty
years has furnished, in proof of the uniform efficacy
and security of the external use of cold water in scarlatina, and in other febrile diseases connected *with
high morbid heat of the skin,* it is to be lamented
that *some practitioners still look upon the practice as
an experiment*; *and repeat the remnants of exploded
hypotheses,* about repelling morbid matter, stopping
pores, etc., as reasons for resisting the testimony of
some of the greatest ornaments of the medical profession.   For my own part, I have been in the con-
stant habit of resorting to the practice at every op-
portunity in scarlatina, (and in other fevers during
my superintendence of the Fever Institute for the last
ten years,) attending to the simple rules laid down
by Dr. Currie, and I have *never* witnessed any incon-
venience, much less any injury from it, *but an uni-
formity in its beneficial operation, of which no other
physical expedient with which I am acquainted af-*

ffords an example." To this, Professor Bock adds, "that any rational treatment of all dyscrasias must look *to supporting properly the metamorphosis and removing troublesome symptoms.*" " Far more patients are restored and quicker strengthened by proper dietetic means than by any drug-medication and stimulation. But a proper dietetic treatment for acute diseases consists in a mild, mostly fluid food; in keeping the air, day and night, fresh and pure; in most scrupulous cleanliness of clothes, bed, and person ; in preventing all excitement; in proper attention to the excretions through the skin by baths; the urinary by the catheter, and the bowels by enemas."

The regular course of small-pox runs through four stages : 1st, *that of the infection;* 2d, *that of the eruption;* 3d, *that of the suppuration*, three days, and 4th, *that of the desquamation.* The whole disease runs from fifteen to sixteen days. With desquamation often appear critical diarrhœas, frequent urine with a puslike sediment, and sometimes salivation. All this proves that the properly managed small-pox is one of the most thoroughly cleansing efforts of nature, and really a health-giving disease, and as such should be treated. The character of the epidemic itself, and the difference in individual constitutions, begets, of course, many anomalies in its manifestations. But the general treatment which under all circumstances I have found perfectly successful, is briefly the following:

As soon as there is the slightest suspicion of the possibility of infection, I rub with wet hands the upper part of the back, thoroughly and repeatedly, in order to so irritate the skin there that the face shall remain free of the eruptions, the virus in the blood always depositing itself by a happy arrangement of Providence, where there is the greatest amount of life and irritation.

The room of the patient must be kept cool, not above 60° Far., and the fever kept within the limits of ordinary eliminative activity by repeated washings with water of 75°. In case the heat is not to be confined by these means, and delirium ensues, we can resort to half-baths of 75°, in which the sufferer remains till he is calmed down, but he must not be chilled; where half-baths are not available, we use wet sheet-packs, repeated according to necessity. If the fever is very violent, we pour water of about 65° F. over the head and shoulders in a half-bath of

70° F.; should the patient be chilly, we must not increase the warmth of the room, but merely cover him more thickly. For drink, we give him only water and a little milk. His food is to consist of light soups, fruit and compots. The bowels are to be kept in order by enemas of 65° F. If the mouth, throat and stomach should be invaded by the eruptions, we apply the usual wet compress to these parts. The irritation of the brain we counteract by packing feet and legs, and giving frequent small enemas of 65°.

The timely rubbing of the back of the neck and between the shoulders with wet hands will prevent the more violent breaking out of the eruptions in the face, which is kept cool by washing with water of 70° F. Larger pustules are soothed by covering them with fine linen kept moist with milk; cream subdues the itching.

Treated in this manner, the small-pox is a blessing, because it frees the body of an immense amount of diseased matters and leaves not a mark behind.

If the medical faculty would emancipate themselves from the blind servitude to drugs, which rarely does more than transpose disease to a less safe place than nature had selected for it, and if they would take the trouble which this treatment requires—for a proper treatment of the small-pox by this process cannot be disposed of by an order made once or twice a day upon an apothecary's shop—they would soon find that small-pox, instead of being regarded as one of our greatest social terrors, would be treated as a providential means of purifying and perfecting our race. They would denounce vaccination with justice, as inoculation was denounced before it, as an interference with the operations of Providence for our good, and would fix the same penalty upon its administrators as is now imposed upon the administration of any other destructive poison.

I close this appeal from drugging to common-sense with the declaration that I am perfectly willing to answer any objections to the contents of the preceding pages, if they are brought forth in a gentlemanly and scientific manner.

DR. SCHIEFERDECKER.

WATER-CURE INSTITUTE,
313 WEST TWENTY-SECOND ST., NEW YORK.

The following pages contain an additional quotation from Dr. Nittinger's work, which seems proper as an appendix to this pamphlet.

Dr. Nittinger exclaims, in a work on "The Evils of Vaccination":

"How rapidly does the scourge progress! The terrible ominous commotion begins already the first, fourth, seventh and ninth day after the vaccination; many, many children fall its victims; and again, others are more fortunate, but mostly some misery remains. The mucous membranes, particularly those of the organs of the senses and generation, (in adults,) attest the sufferings and dangers originating in the inoculated kine-pox poison — ophthalmia, otorrhœa, fluor albus, prurigo, etc.

"What a sea of tears, what an unbounded field of misery lies behind us! Let us add to this the dead, the invalids, the infirm, that come forth out of these struggles! The field on which the battle was so fiercely fought is before us, disordered, ruined, weakened, devastated; it is the extensive *field of digestion and breathing*—the basis, the root of life. Not enough that these terrible traces are re-produced year after

year, but the poisoning goes on again and again, and
poison is heaped into the already poisoned body.
And this is the reason why the affections of the mucous membranes, which were formerly only one-half
of all diseases, have now increased to five-sixths of
their number.   Thou miserable abdomen! thou miserable chest!   Is Pandora's box not yet empty?*

"Gone is all faith in the doctrine of 'not the least
injury.' Nothing has gained but the history of er-
rors and fallacies ; its pages show innumerable new
experiments.   The people have acquired by this
vaccination—

"1. A glorious degree of sickly sensitiveness of the
stomach and intestinal canal, accompanied by open
and hidden disturbances in the whole digestive apparatus, viz: diarrhœa, dyspepsia, phthisis dyspeptica,
liver and spleen suffering, never known before.

"2. An entirely new disease (since 1806) which
domesticates itself every year more firmly, *the typhus*,
which is a mucous fever with ulcerations and pox-
eruptions in the abdominal viscera.

"3. The daily more frequent appearance of a new

---

* Answer:—Not as long as the box of Pandora is the vaccinat-
ing case of instruments.

children-disease, which Millar observed and presented (1755) as the first fruit of inoculation in England—the asthma Millari.

" 4. The poor children have gained, or rather regained, in immensely more malignant form, (since 1806,) the long-before forgotten inflammation of the wind-pipe—croup. As formerly in England nature revolted (1738) against the inoculation of the human small-pox matter and tried valiantly to remove the poison by means of catarrhal gangrenous angina in the throat ; as children for nearly forty years suffered the tortures of horrible strangulation-difficulties, and many thousands of them wretchedly perished; so appears now here and everywhere, where vaccination is introduced, the croup—somewhat milder, because the kine-pox is somewhat milder—and tortures, frightens, sickens, and kills (already some forty years) the innocent victims.

" 5. The whooping cough has gained in strength and extent immensely.

" 6. The human family in general has acquired a monstrous increase in consumptive and hectic diseases, which mostly originate in the digestive apparatus, (phthisis dyspeptica.)

" 7. An entirely new disease, softening of the stomach (v. Jaeger and Camerer) has been added since 1811–1813 to our already immensely large catalogue of destructive diseases.

" 8. Our young women have gained since 1822 a generality of chlorosis and fluor albus, of which we did not dream before.

" 9. The whole human family have been enriched by the acquisition of the Bengalian poison-snake—hydrophis ; the tropical wild-pox poison, the cholera, which now has established itself among us thoroughly and habitually.

" 10. Our generation has, besides all this, gained a far greater susceptibility for the small-pox poison, which will ravage in the above-mentioned diseased forms of the mucous membranes in the interior of the organism, till the feeding of the poison by vaccination, ordered even by laws, sanctioned by the usage, and held up by the faculty, is forbidden under severe penalty. Then only will nature be able to recover all her own ; and then will the external small-pox reappear as a redeeming means for the internal destruction."